Life Skills Every 6 Year Old Should Know

Unlock Your Secret Superpowers and Succeed in All Areas of Life

Hayden Fox

© Copyright - All rights reserved.

Claim your free gifts!

(My way of saying thank you for your support)

Simply visit **haydenfoxmedia.com** to receive the following:

- 10 Powerful Dinner Conversations To Create Amazing Kids

- 10 Magical Affirmations To Help Kids Become Unstoppable in Life

(you can also scan this QR code)

This book belongs to

_____

Table of Contents

Introduction

Hey, kids!

It's so nice to see you here. You're getting so big and I bet you're learning lots of new things each and every day. You know that you go to school to learn, but did you know you can learn lots at home too? That means every day is a chance to learn something new. That's exciting!

This book has lots of new things for you to learn, which means it's going to be super fun and exciting! It's not going to be math or science or how to read though. You will learn other things such as how to be a good person. You will learn about being a good friend. This is a good book to sit down to read with your grown-up. You can talk to your grown-up about the things that you learn. You can have your grown-up help you read the bigger words or even the whole thing if you can't read yet. This is a book that you can read all at once, or you can read one chapter each day or week. When you read a little bit at a time, you can spend extra time practicing each skill before moving to the next one.

The skills in this book aren't always easy. Sometimes, they take lots of practice. But remember, practice makes perfect! The more you practice, the more you learn. The more you learn, the more you can do. And, you are never too old to learn. Everyone is always learning. That's right, even grown-ups are always learning new things. The only difference is that grown-ups have just had more time to learn all the things they do. You will learn in time too.

One of the best ways to learn something new is by reading. You might still be practicing how to read, and that's okay! Lots of kids your age are still learning how to read. But, reading with a grown-up is also a good way to learn how to do new things and can even help you practice your reading.

Remember that when you get stuck on something, it's okay. The grown-ups in your life are there to help. They can talk to you if you get angry or frustrated. They can tell you how they would deal with something. They can even help you solve problems that are too big to solve yourself. You're a big kid now, but even big kids need help sometimes. In fact, even grown-ups need help sometimes too. Don't be afraid to ask for help if you think you need it.

So, are you ready to start learning? Get comfy and let's get started.

Chapter 1: Making a Champion Mindset

Did you know that you have the brain of a champion? We all do. I like to call it a "Champion Mindset." That means you aren't afraid to keep growing and trying to do things, even if you mess up sometimes. That's how champions become champions. When things get hard, they keep trying until they get it right.

It's not always easy. Sometimes, when things get hard, we feel like we want to give up. That's because giving up is easier than choosing to keep trying. When you give up, you don't have to spend any more time on something.

But, when you give up, you don't learn anything. You don't get better at things. That's why the Champion Mindset sets the champions apart. Champions know that the best reward in the whole world is learning and growing. They also know that getting that reward means they have to work hard. It takes effort.

You can have a Champion Mindset too. It's all about how you think and act. It's all about what you do when things get hard.

Story Time!

Johnny is six years old. He likes reading stories, swimming, and going to the park to play with his friends. Johnny really wants to learn how to play piano, just like his best friend. He has heard his friend play piano and thinks it will be easy. So, Johnny's grown-ups sign him up for piano classes. Once a week, he goes to learn from a teacher.

The first time he sits down, he doesn't know what the keys are. He doesn't know how to read the music. He doesn't know how to tell which sounds are which notes. His first lesson is really hard. He goes home sad that he can't play piano like his friend does. He couldn't even remember one note!

When Johnny goes home, he wants to quit. He tells his grown-ups that he hates it. He's no good at it and he'll never be able to do what his friend does.

Johnny's grown-ups tell him that he can't quit after just one try. They say that he has to try for two months because he signed up for two months of classes. After two months, he can choose to quit.

At first, Johnny doesn't like it cause it's so hard. But, after a few weeks, he starts to learn where the keys are. He learns how to play *Twinkle Twinkle Little Star!* After two months go by, his grown-ups ask if he still wants to quit. Johnny says no. He wants to keep going and learning because it's getting easier!

Don't Give Up When Things Are Hard

Johnny wanted to give up because playing piano is hard. It's hard for grown-ups to learn too! He kept practicing because his grown-ups said he needed to try for more than one day, and he started to learn. Every lesson, it got a little bit easier.

When something is hard for you, remember that if you keep trying, you will learn. Don't decide that you will never be able to do it. Tell yourself that you can't do it yet, but you know you will learn. This helps you think positively. It helps you keep trying toward your goals.

Try New Things When You Are Stuck

When you get stuck on something, do you keep trying the same way you tried before? Or do you try new things instead? Sometimes, trying again the way you did it the first time can help you if you are stuck because you made a mistake somewhere. For example, maybe you are doing math homework and have to solve 4 + 9. If you count wrong the first time, counting a second time could give you the right answer.

But for many things, when something you try doesn't work, it means that you need to try again in a different way. For example, if you are trying to make green paint and choose to mix blue and red, you will get purple. No matter how much blue and red you mix, you won't ever get green. Trying a different strategy, like mixing blue and yellow instead, will get you what you want.

If you are stuck on something, think about asking for help or advice. Your grown-up may be able to make suggestions. For example, maybe you always fight with your friend because you always want to play tag but your friend always wants to play superheroes. You argue about what to play and neither of you wants to give in. Your grown-up might say that you should choose a different game that you both like. When you do that, you stop fighting so much.

You can try new things in other ways too. Maybe you are trying to make slime but it keeps coming out wrong. If you change how much of each part you mix, you might get a different result.

Chapter 2: Tattling and Telling

Have you ever tattled on someone? Tattling isn't the same as telling a grown-up when there's something wrong or bad happening. Kids tattle for lots of reasons. Sometimes, they want to make the other kid look bad. They do this because they think it can make them feel better. Other times, they might tattle because they want to get the other person in trouble.

The problem with tattling is that not everything that happens needs a grown-up to help. When you tattle and get a grown-up involved, you take that grown-up away from something else they should be doing. The other problem is that if kids tattle just to get someone in trouble and not because they could get hurt, they are bullying the other person.

Sometimes, telling a grown-up that something is happening is the right thing to do, and sometimes, it's better to let the kids figure it out on their own. After all, we learn from our mistakes!

Story Time!

Val sees Alex and David hiding under the playground eating candy at recess. She knows the school rules say that all food has to be eaten at the table. Val decides to go to the teacher who is watching the kids play outside and tells about Alex and David eating candy. The teacher goes and makes the two kids sit out for the rest of recess for breaking the rules.

Later, Alex sees Val doodling in class instead of doing her work. Alex raises his hand and tells the teacher. Val is told to focus on her work and feels very embarrassed. Alex and Val always tell on each other when they see the other one not following the rules.

One day, Val sees Alex trying to climb on the outside of the playground at recess. She goes to tell the teacher, but the teacher tells her that she's told on Alex too much. Because she has tattled so many times, the teacher doesn't listen. Alex falls off the playground and gets hurt. He has to go home and comes back to school a few days later with a cast on his arm. Val tattled so much that when she tried to tell about something dangerous, the teacher didn't pay attention.

Know the Difference Between Tattling and Telling

In the story, Val and Alex both tattled a lot. That tattling meant that the teacher didn't really believe them when something serious was happening. Yes, both Val and Alex were pointing out times when the other wasn't following the rules. Sometimes, it's better to let someone solve the problems they create by themselves so they can learn.

Telling is important when there is something dangerous happening. When Val told on Alex for climbing up the playground, she made the right choice because Alex could, and did, get hurt. There are a lot of situations where it's the right choice to speak up. If you are afraid that the person breaking the rules could get hurt or could hurt someone else, or if you are scared, telling a grown-up is the right choice.

For example, let's say you're sitting at a table for lunch and the kid sitting next to you touches your lunchbox. You might be angry about it, but a teacher probably won't do anything except remind the other kid to keep their hands to themselves. It is better if you try yourself to tell the other kid to leave your lunchbox alone.

However, if the kid next to you doesn't stop or takes your lunchbox instead, it's okay to go to the grown-up and tell. When someone takes your food, it's harmful because you need to eat to stay healthy. Taking your lunch is bullying you. A teacher or other grown-up can help.

What to Do Instead of Tattling

Just because you shouldn't tattle doesn't mean that it's okay to break the rules, even if it's not dangerous. Rules are usually there for a reason. Some keep us safe or healthy. Others help create fairness. Rules help us to live together in groups with fewer problems. People live in big groups, which we call society. Our society is our community. It's you, your family, your neighbors, and all the other people who live around you.

When you know that someone isn't following the rules, but they aren't going to hurt themselves or someone else, it's okay to remind them of what they should be doing. It's not okay to try to force them to follow the rules because you aren't the one in charge.

If they still won't follow the rules after a reminder, it's time to think about whether it's important to go tell a grown-up, or if it's okay to let them break the rules and deal with the consequences later. Alex might have been eating candy on the playground, but that also means he may have a tummy ache later. Val might have been doodling instead of working, but that could mean that she has to miss free time because her work isn't done.

Chapter 3: How To Make Connections

Did you know that you can make connections with anyone or anything? It's one of the easiest ways to learn about people and ideas. When you make connections between ideas, you find ways to tie what you know to something new.

When you connect with people, you get to know them. You might even make new life-long friends!

I like making connections when I'm learning something new because it helps me to remember everything. Maybe you know how to play soccer, but you want to learn how to play a new sport. You can find ways to connect what you know about soccer to what you're learning now.

Story Time!

Molly is learning about growing plants in school. She really loves it. Her teacher tells the class about how seeds sprout and turn into big plants that make food with the sun, and that they grow flowers to make more seeds. Her class does a big project where they each get to plant a seed and take care of it until it grows.

Molly loves plants because her grandpa has a big vegetable garden. Every summer, she gets to help him take care of the plants and watch them grow. Her favorite part is picking the fruits and veggies and making delicious recipes with them. Her grandpa says food always tastes better when you grow it yourself.

In class, Molly is very excited to grow her own plant all by herself. One day, after the plants have started to sprout, her friend Ella's plant looks a little droopy. It looks a little yellowish. All the other plants are standing up big and strong, but Ella's plant seems too small. Ella looks sadly at her plant and says she doesn't know what's wrong.

Molly smiles. Ella looks confused. Then, Molly tells her that when she helped her grandpa over the summer, one of the plants grew like that. It was getting too much water and couldn't grow right.

Ella tries watering her plant less, and soon it's green and happy, just like the others.

Making Connections Between Ideas

In the story, Molly helps Ella because she makes a connection between something she has seen before and what she sees in class. She connects her real-life experiences with a new experience, and it helps her to fix the problem.

When you make connections between ideas, you take what you know to learn more about the next topic. It's something that people do a lot when they read stories. If you read a story and feel like you and a character have something in common, you've made a connection. For example, maybe the main character in your book has a big brother who teases them sometimes, but they love each other. If you have a big sister who picks on you sometimes, but you both love each other, you can relate to the main character.

You can make connections with ideas in three ways. You can relate to the idea yourself, like with the big brother example. You can also relate the idea to another idea or book, like with relating soccer to baseball. The last big way you can make connections is by relating an idea to the world. Maybe there was a big storm that knocked down a bunch of trees in your town. When you watch a movie that has a big tree fall over and break something, you can connect to that.

To make a connection between two ideas, you can say, "When that happened, it reminded me of..." and then fill in the rest. It's that easy to make a connection between ideas! Try it the next time you watch a movie or read a story. Find a way to connect between the two.

Making Connections With People

Think about your best friend. Why do you like them so much? Is it because you like all the same things? Is it because your friend is funny or smart? Did you like your friend when you first met, or did you start liking them when you got to know them?

We get to know people by making connections. We find ways that we are similar and those let us bond. The people you meet will be different from you. That's normal. Even though people are different, they can still connect.

We all eat. We all sleep. We all want to belong. Even if everything else about someone is different, there are always similarities. When you talk to someone new, find ways you can relate to each other.

If you see ways that you and the other person are different, remember it's okay to disagree. You can still be friends with someone who has different likes, thoughts, and beliefs. You can be friends with someone who speaks a different language or follows a different religion. All you need to do is find ways to relate to each other.

Chapter 4: Waiting Quietly While Grown-Ups Talk

Sometimes, grown-ups stop to talk. Maybe they have to speak to the doctor after your check-up, or they might talk to a friend they see at the store. It can be really boring when grown-ups are busy talking, especially if you don't have anything to do. Regardless, you have to be patient.

Learning to sit quietly while grown-ups talk can help in other ways too. If you can wait patiently while grown-ups talk, you can also wait in class, in the car, while standing in line somewhere, or anywhere. You can wait your turn to talk so you don't interrupt someone else. It's a good skill to have because a lot of time is spent waiting as you grow up.

Story Time!

Aiden likes to talk. A lot. He chats with his mom at the store while they grocery shop. They talk about what kinds of foods they want to eat and about their days. One day, Aiden and his mom walk into the store. When they're choosing bread, his mom's friend comes up. Aiden is really annoyed because he likes to talk to his mom, but now, he has to stand there and wait!

It feels like his mom is talking *forever*. Aiden gets bored and starts asking if they can leave. Aiden's mom shushes him and tells him that she's talking and that he needs to wait a few minutes. Aiden *hates* waiting. It's so boring to stand around and do nothing.

Aiden decides to poke at the bread on the shelf. Then he pokes another and another. Soon, he's poked in the middle of lots of loaves of bread!

Aiden's mom notices and tells him that he shouldn't have done that. She tells him that it's not okay to ruin things just because he has to wait. Aiden feels bad about ruining the bread and says he just wanted to find something to do.

Play a Quiet Game by Yourself

If you're like Aiden, you don't like to wait either. It's easy to get distracted by something when you're standing around. That's because your brain isn't done growing yet. When you see something that seems interesting, you might have a hard time controlling yourself. It's harder for kids to control themselves than it is for grown-ups, and sometimes, waiting is hard for grown-ups too.

One thing you can do when you have to wait is to find a way to make it fun. Aiden tried to do this, but made a bad choice when he started poking at the bread. That's because poking at the bread made it smush down in the middle. That means that people would be buying bread that had been damaged if they took one of those loaves.

When you have to wait, you need to find something to do that's a good choice. That means that it can't go against the rules that you have to follow. It also has to not break, ruin, or hurt anyone or anything.

Before you decide on something to do, you need to stop and think. Ask yourself if something bad will happen if you do it. If nothing bad will happen and it doesn't break the rules or hurt someone, it could be a good choice.

Talk to your grown-up to think of some quiet ways you can wait. One thing I like to do when I have to wait is to play the alphabet game. To play, you have to find something around you that starts with every letter of the alphabet. You start with A and look around. Maybe in the bread aisle, Aiden saw an apple pie. Then, find something that starts with B. There's lots of bread around Aiden. Next, you look for something with the letter C. Aiden might look up at the ceiling. Keep playing through all the letters. It's kind of like playing "I Spy" and a puzzle all in one.

Plan Ahead and Pack Something

It's always a good idea to be prepared. If you have a chatty grown-up and wait a lot, you can always pack some small, quiet things to bring along when you go somewhere you might have to wait. You could bring a little notepad and a pencil so you can draw or write a story, or a small, quiet toy to play with. I like to bring books with me when I know I'll be waiting around. Ask your grown-up if you can put some small things in a backpack, or see if they can put them in their purse or pocket for you.

Only Interrupt if It's Important!

Sometimes, you might need to interrupt your grown-up while they're talking. When something dangerous is happening, you are hurt, or you need important help right that minute, you might need to interrupt. That's okay! What's important is that you do it politely. Maybe have a special touch or hand signal you use with your grown-up to tell them you need to talk to them. You can also politely say, "Excuse me" to get their attention.

Chapter 5: Respecting Personal Bubbles

Are you a big hugger or do you like it when people don't touch you?

Your body belongs to you. That means that you can say yes when people want to touch you or give you a hug, or you can say no. The same is true for everyone else in the world. If you don't want a hug, you probably wouldn't like it if someone tried to make you give them one. The same goes for other people too.

Everyone has a personal bubble. That's their personal space. It's their body, plus the space right around them. You can get really close to someone without touching them, but a lot of people don't like that. That's why it's so important to respect personal bubbles.

Story Time!

Penny hates it when her sister, Violet, touches her hair. Violet likes all things fluffy and soft, so hair is one of her favorite things to touch. Every time Violet touches Penny's hair, Penny feels angry. She yells at Violet to stop touching her and tells her to leave her alone.

Their mom always says that Violet needs to respect Penny's space. Violet says sorry, but always does it again when she sees Penny run by with her hair in pigtails.

One day, Violet reaches for Penny's hair. Penny tells her to stop it! Violet stops right before touching Penny's hair, and Penny tells her to move. Violet smiles and says, "But I'm not touching you."

Violet learns that she can make Penny mad without ever touching her. She starts getting extra close to Penny and reaching for her hair without touching it. Penny feels even angrier than she did when Violet touched her hair.

Remember, Bubbles Pop if You Get Too Close

Think about a bubble for a minute. Bubbles might look nice and be fun to chase, but when you touch one, it pops, even if you're gentle with it. If you don't want a bubble to pop, you need to give it space.

If you don't want to make people angry, you need to give them space too.

Part of why Penny gets so angry at Violet even when Violet doesn't touch her is that she feels like her personal space isn't respected. That's because Violet pops her personal bubble. Violet is getting so close to Penny that Penny feels uncomfortable.

Most people like to have some space from others around them. It's nice to be able to move around and not feel like you are going to bump into someone else. People might like hugs and cuddles, but they don't like them all the time. I'm sure there are times when you don't want to be touched, and that's okay! You are always allowed to say you want space.

One thing that can help you remember to give other people enough personal space is to remember their bubble. Imagine that bubble around every other person and remind yourself that touching them will make the bubble pop. When you start getting close to someone when they don't want you to, remembering to protect their bubble can be a reminder that helps.

Ask Before You Touch

Not everyone wants to be touched or hugged. Some people never want hugs and other people want to hug everyone they care about. If you are a hugger, but your best friend hates touch, it can feel hard to keep yourself from hugging them. If you're not a hugger, it can feel bad to be touched by other people. So, how do you find a balance?

The answer is asking. Before you reach to give your friend a hug, you should say, "Can I give you a hug?" If they say yes, then you can give it to them. If they say no, you need to respect their bubble. When someone says yes to being touched, you can touch them without popping their bubble. When they say no, touching them anyway makes their bubble pop, and that hurts their feelings.

Imagine a Hula-Hoop

If you're not sure how much space you should give other people when they don't want to be touched, you can think of Hula-Hoops. If you were playing with a Hula-Hoop, would you hit the other person with it? If you would, it's time to give them some more space. This works because it gives you something that you can imagine to understand how much space should be between you and the other person.

Chapter 6: Remembering Important Things

Have you ever forgotten something? Maybe you were super excited to go to school because it was show-and-tell day. You ran out the door, got on the bus, and when you got to school, you realized you'd forgotten to bring what you wanted to share. Or, you could forget a very important chore, like feeding your pet.

Sometimes, forgetting something isn't very important. If you forgot that you wanted to wear your favorite shirt for picture day, there isn't a lot of bad that can happen. If you forgot your homework or your lunch, you might be in a little bit of trouble.

Everyone forgets things sometimes. It's normal, but it can be really frustrating when you forget something important. Important things really need to get done, so working on ways to remember them can help. Remembering things can help you at school, at home, and with your friends.

Story Time!

Amy is very forgetful. She'd forget her own feet if they weren't attached to her legs! She forgets when her friends' birthdays are and forgets to do her part when working as a group. One time, she even forgot to get dressed in the morning and got on the school bus in her pajama shirt!

Amy's friend, Jenny, is having a movie sleepover party for her birthday. Amy is invited and Jenny reminds her that it's very important that they all dress up like a character from the movie they're going to watch.

Amy is so excited for the sleepover party! She packs all her things, even her stuffed puppy she sleeps with every night. She remembers her toothbrush, her sleeping bag, and her pajamas.

When she gets to Jenny's house, she waves goodbye to her dad and runs inside.

Then, she remembers.

She was supposed to be dressed up! She looks at all her other friends and they're all dressed in costumes. Amy is the only one wearing her normal clothes. Amy is so embarrassed and starts to cry. She decides that she wants to go home. She doesn't tell her dad why she decided not to stay at the sleepover. She stays in her room, feeling sad, wondering why she forgets so many things.

Take Notes

When there's something important to remember, you might tell yourself it will be fine. But, if you tend to forget, one of the easiest ways to remember is to take notes. I take notes about important things like appointments, meetings, and things I need to do. Amy could have taken a note about wearing a costume for the party. If you can't spell the word, it's okay! Use your best guess to spell the word. Or, you could draw a little picture of the item or thing you need to remember.

Taking notes helps you in two ways. First, when you write something down, your brain can remember it better. It remembers better because the more you repeat something, the easier it is to make it a memory. The second way it helps is that when you take a note of what you need to do, you can go back to that note later when you think you've forgotten something, but you don't know what you forgot.

Use a Rhyme, Song, or Silly Phrase

If you're having a hard time remembering something you're learning in school, you can try using a silly phrase, song, or rhyme that helps you remember. This is called using a mnemonic (ne-mon-ick). That's a big, silly-looking word that means something that helps you remember.

One that you might have heard can help you remember which way to turn a lid to open it: "Righty, tighty. Lefty, loosey." By making it a rhyme, it's easier for you to remember, so when you need to know which way to turn a lid, you repeat it to yourself.

You can make your own silly phrases to help you remember too. For example, as Amy needed to wear a costume to her sleepover, she could have said, "Dress your best to get some rest." That would remind her that she needed certain clothes for her sleepover. When there's something you need to remember, get creative with how to keep it in mind.

Chapter 7: Working Together

There's a reason people say teamwork makes the dream work! When people work together, they can do great things. Let's say you want to build a giant sandcastle. You have two big buckets and two shovels. Building the sandcastle will go more quickly if you have someone else working with you because you can each fill a bucket at the same time. That's double the sand ready to go at the same time! Now, imagine there are four people filling buckets at the same time. That's even more sand!

There are lots of times when you'll have to work with others. You'll have group projects at school. Your whole family works together at home to take care of things. When you're a grown-up, you'll probably have to work as a team at your job. But, it's not always easy to work with other people. Sometimes, things won't go how you want them to. Other times, you'll have to listen to what other people say you should do. You can't always be the leader, so you need to be able to work on what you are told to do, even if you think you want to do things differently.

Story Time!

Noah is very confident. He loves being in charge and deciding how to do things. When Noah joins a soccer team, he wants to be the one to score all the goals. He doesn't think about the other people on his team. He tries to hog the ball and doesn't pass it when he should. Noah's team misses a lot of goals because Noah doesn't pass the ball.

Noah's team gets frustrated. They talk about how to play together. They talk about how it's important to work as a team because any goals scored are goals for everyone. Soon, Noah's teammates stop passing him the ball. Noah feels frustrated because he can't play the way he wants to.

Noah's coach has a talk with him. Noah's coach explains that if Noah doesn't work together with the rest of the team, then he's hurting everyone. When Noah's teammates kick the ball to anyone else on the team, they know that they can trust their teammates, but they can't trust Noah. The coach says that Noah has to be willing to share the ball if he wants to be included.

Noah listens to his coach. He talks to his teammates. They agree that they have to share the ball, even if that means they let someone else get the goal because sometimes, someone else is somewhere better to kick it. They talk about a plan.

At the next game, Noah plays well. He shares the ball. At the end of the game, he has the ball, but he sees that he can't get to the goal by himself. He kicks the ball to his teammate and his teammate scores the goal. His team wins!

Talk Together to Make a Plan Everyone Agrees With

When you have to work as a team, it's important that everyone is on the same page. That means everyone knows what they have to do, how they have to do it, and when it will be finished. This means coming up with a plan. Your group should work together to find the best way to divide the work.

You might not get your first pick of jobs, just like Noah didn't when he had to share the ball or kick it to someone else. But, when everyone plays their part, the whole project comes together. Be willing to do the parts you might not like as much. You'll help everyone, and maybe the next time you'll get the part you want.

Know What You're Good At

Part of making a plan on what to do is knowing what everyone on the team is good at and what is hard. If you have to make a big poster for a project with a group, each person will have to do part of it. Maybe you have very good handwriting and your partner is good at drawing, so you put all the writing on the poster and your partner does the drawings. Another partner might be good at investigating, so they figure out what needs to be included. Another one might be really good at organizing things, so they keep track of what needs to be done and make sure all the pieces come together. When you all bring your strengths to the table, you can do your best work. This lets everyone shine.

Chapter 8: Being a Good Sport

Winning can be a lot of fun, but it isn't everything there is in the world.

When you win, you can feel really good about yourself. Losing is never very fun, and can feel really bad. We all lose sometimes. You might play a video game with your friend and they're much better at it than you. You could be playing a game in class and the other team does better. There are lots of times when we lose, and that's okay.

When you lose, it's important to be a good sport about it. That means that you accept that you lost and you don't get angry or throw a fit about it. It can be hard sometimes, especially if losing made you feel really bad, but it's important. If everyone played a fair game and you lost, then you lost. You can learn and try again another time.

Story Time!

Brody and his sister Layla love to play board games together. They are very competitive.

Brody wins sometimes and Layla wins other times. When they get a new game, Layla starts winning almost all the time. Brody gets frustrated. He thinks about cheating to win. He thinks about never playing the game again.

One day, they're playing the game and Brody is winning. He's so excited! But then, at the last minute, Layla beats him. Brody is furious! He throws the game off the table, screams that Layla cheated, and storms off to his room.

Brody gets in trouble for his bad behavior. His dad comes to talk to him and says he's not being a good sport. His dad says that he needs to be a good sport if he wants people to play with him. He explains it's not fun to play with a bad sport.

Play Fair

The most important part of being a good sport is playing fair. That means there's no cheating involved. When everyone plays a game by the rules, it's more fun for everyone. That's important because playing games should be fun. Make sure everyone playing the game knows what the rules are and chooses to play by them.

If you think someone isn't playing fair, it's a good idea to talk to a coach or a trusted grown-up. The rules are there to be followed, especially if you are in sports or team activities. This is different from tattling because when people don't play fair, they hurt everyone else. Lying and cheating are never okay.

Be Positive

Another important part of being a good sport is being positive even when you lose. It's okay to be disappointed. It's not okay to yell and say people are cheating. When you lose, try doing these things to stay positive:

- Tell yourself that you gave it a good try and tried your best.

- Treat the other person or team with respect. Don't yell at them or call them names.

- Shake hands with the other player or team.

- Instead of thinking about who won or lost, think about what you did well and what you could do better next time.

- Tell the winning team they did a good job.

Be Kind When You Win

Being a good sport is something winners have to do too. When you win, do you laugh at the other team and say things like, "In your face! We totally wrecked you!"? It can be tempting, especially after getting a hard win, but this isn't very good sportsmanship.

When you win, it's okay to be proud of yourself and to celebrate. It's not okay to brag or tease the losing team. When people play together, it's important that they show respect for each other, whether they win or lose. Instead of teasing the other team, tell them it was a good game.

Don't Argue With the Results

When Brody lost against his sister, he said that she cheated. He argued about the results of the game. He didn't really think Layla cheated, but he was embarrassed and upset that he lost. It's okay to be angry if someone cheats, but if you have no proof, you shouldn't tell them that they did. When Brody told Layla that she cheated, he was saying she couldn't win fair and square when she did.

When the game ends, the results show you who wins. Don't tell the judge or referee that they are wrong. If everyone played fair, then the results are what they are. As long as you tried your best, you should be proud of yourself!

Chapter 9: How to Give Directions

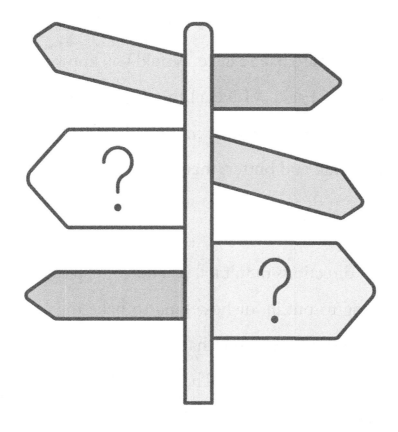

Have you ever made a really cool project and someone asked you how you did it? Or have you ever tried to help someone with something? When someone wants to do what you did and asks you how you did it, you give them directions.

Giving directions isn't always easy. Let's say you want to bake a cake. Would you know what to do if I said, "Take all the flour and salt and dry stuff and throw it in a bowl with the eggs and milk and butter, then bake it"?

Probably not!

My directions didn't tell you how much of each thing to put in, or how long to bake the cake. They don't even say that you need to mix the ingredients together! That's an example of bad directions. Giving bad directions can make it hard for other people to do things the right way.

Giving directions is an important thing to know how to do because it happens a lot. You might be teaching a friend how to play a game or do something with you. Or, you could need to help a teammate learn something for school. When you are a grown-up and go to work, you will probably have to give directions then too. That's why it's so important to start learning how to do it now. By the time you really need the skill, you'll have lots of practice and be a direction-giving pro!

Story Time!

Connor and his friend, Zane, are working on building their very own catapult. They have all their crafting sticks, rubber bands, spoons, and everything else they think they will need. Connor makes his catapult very quickly. He's done the project before and knew what he was doing. He goes off to start launching marshmallows.

Zane, on the other hand, gets stuck. He can't figure out how to put the pieces together. Connor tries telling him what to do from across the room: "You just rubber-band the sticks together and they launch the marshmallows!" Zane tries and tries but can't figure it out. He gets frustrated and gives up.

Be Specific

When you give directions to someone, you have to be specific. You need to tell them how to do it step by step. Don't just say, "Put the rubber bands on the stick," show them how to do it. Point to where the rubber bands go. This helps the other person figure out what they are doing. The more specific you can be, the better.

To help you be specific, imagine that you are talking about every step as you do them. "First, I put the sticks together in a stack. Then I rubber band them on the end. Make sure the rubber band is really tight so it holds in place."

Get Close to the Other Person

When we talk to people, we usually do it standing near each other. This helps us to talk and understand each other clearly. There are fewer distractions when you stand next to someone to talk. It's easier to hear the words. And, you can feel like you have a connection with the other person. All of this makes it easier to communicate. When you give directions to someone, you are communicating with them. Would you like it if you asked a grown-up how to make something and they just yelled at you across the room? Probably not! I know I wouldn't.

When you are helping someone else with instructions, don't shout the instructions from across the room! It's really easy to get things mixed up when you try to listen to someone talk when they're too far away. When you're giving directions to someone, you should stand next to them so you can talk closely. Make sure that you give the other person your full attention. Put down your toy or whatever else you have and look at the other person. Make it a conversation and take the time to really teach them.

Give Instructions Slowly and One at a Time

You might want to rush through all the instructions really quickly so you can go do something else. This doesn't help the other person very much though. If someone told you five things all at once and then walked away, would you remember what they said?

The best way to give instructions is to do it slowly and to give the steps one by one. Think about building LEGOs or following a how-to-draw guide. When you build LEGOs, you look at the steps one at a time. When you follow a video showing you how to draw something, you can pause it between steps so you can take your time and focus. When you give instructions slowly and one at a time, it helps the other person really understand what they are doing and keeps them from forgetting something or messing something up.

Ask If There Are Any Questions

When you are teaching someone, it's always a good idea to ask them if they have any questions while you go. Sometimes, people don't understand exactly what the instructions mean or need a little extra explanation. That's okay! We all learn at our own pace. Don't get frustrated when the other person asks questions. And, if you can, remember to ask them along the way if they have any questions, especially if they look like they are stuck.

Chapter 10: How to Be Curious

The whole world is full of all sorts of wonders. Why is the sky blue? Why do so many animals walk on four legs when people walk on two? How are stars so big when they look so small in the sky? How are rainbows made?

As a kid still learning how the world works, you probably have a lot of questions about the world around you, and that's great! Learning is a lifelong journey. That's right, even grown-ups have things they learn. There's no one in the world who knows every single thing about it.

Being curious is something that some kids stop doing. Maybe they ask so many questions that they're told not to ask as many. Or, they might not like feeling that they don't know something. Being curious is a very good skill to have because when you're curious about the world, you always learn something new. When you learn something new, you grow. That's how you get a Champion Mindset! When you know that there's always more to learn, you are always making yourself better, each and every day.

Story Time!

Kelly loves to learn. All the time, she has questions about the world. She wants to know why water freezes and how fires work. She asks her grown-ups more questions than she can count. Whenever a question pops into her mind, she has to ask it right away.

One day, Kelly's mom is on the phone downstairs. Kelly yells for her mom and her mom comes running. Her mom is afraid there is something wrong. When Kelly's mom comes into the room, Kelly asks why the lightbulbs glow.

Kelly's mom isn't very happy that she was interrupted. She's also not very happy that Kelly didn't get up and go to her to ask the question. She explains that it's good to ask questions, but it's not okay to yell about them. When Kelly's mom calms down, she tells Kelly to think about her question and see if she can come up with an answer, and that they can research it together later.

Before You Ask, Think About Your Answer

It's okay to have questions. Grown-ups do all the time. How many times have you seen your grown-up reach for their phone or computer to type in a question? It probably happens lots of times a day and you never even notice it! Asking questions is good because it helps you learn.

Before you ask a question, though, it's a good idea to try to solve it yourself. This is how scientists think. Before scientists start an experiment or go looking for an answer, they have a hypothesis (hi-poth-ih-sis). That's a very big word that basically means an educated guess. You can come up with your own guesses too by making connections with what you know.

Maybe you want to know how bumblebees fly when their wings are so small. You think about how birds fly by flapping their wings. You might know that birds are very light, and they use their big wings and feathers to catch the wind and lift them up. But, bees don't have big wings or feathers to catch the wind. You might decide that maybe, bees fly like hummingbirds. They flap their wings so quickly that they can fly in the air. You make the connection between hummingbirds and bees and use that for your answer.

Once you have an answer you think is right, you can ask a grown-up to help you learn about it. Sometimes, you'll be right, and other times, you'll be wrong. But, when your answer is wrong, that means you've learned something new and that's great!

Ask the Right Questions at the Right Time

When you have a question, you might want to ask it right away. Sometimes, this is fine. Maybe you're talking to your grown-up about gardening. Your grown-up explains that bees help flowers by spreading pollen. While you are having the talk, you can ask about how bees fly because it's part of what you are already talking about. If your grown-up is talking about what you'll be doing over the weekend and letting you know what chores you have, interrupting to ask about how bees fly probably isn't a good idea. It's rude and makes it seem like you aren't paying attention.

Sometimes, it's better to wait a little bit and ask the question at the right time. Maybe you're in class and your teacher is reading you a story about bees and flowers. You might want to raise your hand and ask right away, but then you would be interrupting the story. You could be at home while your grown-up is on the phone when you come up with your question. It's not a good idea to interrupt them when they're busy.

The best time to ask a question is when there's a break. If you are in school, you could ask the question after your story is done. At home, it could be after your grown-up gets off the phone. Wait for the grown-up to not be busy, then ask it.

If you are worried about forgetting the question, you can use the skills for remembering important things. Write it down or come up with something that will remind you to ask. If you're worried about waiting so long to ask, remember your skills for waiting quietly.

Experiment and See What Happens

Another great way to learn is to experiment. Make sure you talk to your grown-up before deciding to do an experiment because not all experiments are safe. For example, you should never mix cleaners together to see what happens because sometimes they can make things that are poisonous. Other experiments are very messy and your grown-ups might not be very happy.

If you have a question and you want to test it, coming up with an experiment can give you a lot of information. It'd be pretty hard to do an experiment on bees and hummingbirds, but maybe you want to know what would happen if a seed got planted somewhere dark. You could put a seed in a little paper cup with soil and hide it in a cabinet to see what happens. Experiments are fun, and they are a great way to grow your thinking brain and your science skills!

Chapter 11: How to Take Charge

Are you good at being a leader? It's not easy.

Being a leader means that you have a lot of responsibility on your plate. It means that you have to work harder. It's not enough to just tell someone what to do. You have to make them *want* to do it. You have to know what has to happen and find a way to get everyone to work together.

It's not something that everyone likes to do either. Even though it might not be your favorite thing to lead, it's something that everyone should know how to do. Sometimes, you might end up leading because you're the right choice for the job. When you are older, you might babysit for someone, and you'll need to know how to get people to follow you.

Story Time!

Brooke is great at following directions. When it's her turn to be in charge, she loves it. She likes being in control. But, no one ever wants to listen to her. When she tells people what to do, they sometimes call her Bossy Brooke because they don't like how she tries to lead.

At recess, Brooke wants to play a game she made up. She starts telling everyone the rules and what they have to do. When they start playing, she says that everyone is doing it wrong. No one has any fun playing because she stops everyone and tells them to do things differently so much. Soon, everyone goes off to play something else and leaves Brooke all alone.

Brook is disappointed and sad. She asks everyone why they're not playing with her. No one wants to tell her. After Brooke asks and asks, one person comes up and quietly says it's no fun playing with her because she's too bossy. She says that if Brooke were a little bit nicer during playtime, more people would want to play. She also says that everyone would like it more if Brooke took turns with other people being the leader sometimes too, because they want to choose what to do sometimes. It's not fair if Brooke is always in charge.

Brooke has two choices. She can keep playing how she always plays, or she can listen to her friend. She thinks about it for a long time and ponders about how she would feel if other people treated her that way. She wouldn't like it at all.

Motivating Your Team

Brooke's problem is that she gets too bossy. She wants everything done exactly her way. Anything else isn't good enough. When people do something differently, she gets angry at them and tells them that she's in charge so they have to do what she says.

Brooke isn't very good at motivating her team.

When you want people to follow you, you have to *earn* it. It's not enough to just have the title of being in charge. This means that you can't just expect people to do what you want. By being a good leader, you motivate people to follow you. A good leader is

- kind

- honest

- a good listener and decision-maker

- willing to help others

- encouraging

People will follow you if you show them that you care. They will want to help you if you help them. Think about everyone else in your group when you are leading. Listen to what they think and say, and pay attention to them.

Plan Your Goal and How to Get There

You can't lead if there's nowhere to go! When you're leading other people, there has to be some sort of goal. You could be trying to play a game together or working on a project. Everyone needs to know what has to be done, and that means, as the leader, it's your job to figure it out.

Think about what the goal is for everyone. Do you need to build something? Will you be playing together? Once you know what the end goal is, you can start planning the way there.

When you have a goal, it's kind of like looking at a map. You know where you are now, and you know where you want to go. The key is figuring out how to get there. It can feel like a puzzle sometimes. That's why working together is so important.

Talk to the people on your team about what they think your group should do. Have a brainstorming session. This means that everyone says all the ideas they can think of. It doesn't matter what it is. You can figure out if it's a good idea later.

Once you have a list of ideas, you can decide as a group which one is best. This helps everyone feel heard. It shows that you care about what the other people in your group think.

Chapter 12: How to Empower Yourself

A big part of having a Champion Mindset is knowing that you can do whatever you set your mind to. It's being able to remind yourself that even if you can't do something now, you can learn how. This is called empowering yourself.

When you empower yourself, you remind yourself of how good, strong, and smart you are.

It's not always easy to empower yourself. Sometimes, you might want to quit when things are hard. Sometimes, you might think that it really is impossible to do what you're trying to do. But remember that Champion Mindset! You can do anything if you keep trying and keep learning. Giving up is easy. Working hard and learning new things isn't.

Story Time!

Oliver has big dreams. He wants to get his yellow belt in karate. He's worked hard learning all the moves, and he thinks he can do them.

But, there's one thing he's afraid of about his test: He has to break a board.

Oliver worries he won't be strong enough to break the board. He spends a lot of time thinking about what would happen if he can't break it. He's afraid that he will fail and he won't get his yellow belt. He's afraid he'll never be able to get the yellow belt because he might never be strong enough.

At dinner, the night before the test, Oliver looks sad. His mom asks him what's wrong. Oliver tells her all about what's worrying him. Oliver's mom reminds him that it's okay to fail sometimes. And, just because he fails one time doesn't mean he'll fail again the next time he tries. She reminds him that as long as he tries his best and doesn't give up, he can do anything.

Oliver feels a little better after talking to his mom. When he goes to his test, he reminds himself to do his best. He tells himself that he can do it. When he kicks the board, it breaks! He did it and he got his yellow belt. He was worried about something that never even happened!

Always Try Your Best

It's normal to worry about what you can and can't do. What's important is remembering to try your best. If you do your best, you can be proud of yourself. No one can get everything right every single time. It's just part of growing as a person. But, if we all got everything perfectly correct the first time, don't you think things would be boring? What fun would it be to do something if you can already do it exactly right? Part of the fun of learning is seeing yourself grow and get better.

Think about it this way too. If you're in math, how good would you feel if you solved 1 + 2? That's probably really easy for you. What if I told you to solve 132 + 368? That looks a lot harder and takes a lot more skill. You'd probably feel better and more accomplished doing something that made you work harder than getting something easy correct on your first guess.

To try your best, you have to believe in yourself. If you don't believe in yourself, it's going to be hard to give your best effort. People who think they can't do something don't try as hard because it feels like they're wasting their time. Remember that you can do anything with enough practice and effort. You can grow. It's okay to not be perfect at everything you do.

Make Your Own Catchphrases

A really fun thing that I like to do to empower myself is use catchphrases. These are things that I tell myself when I'm feeling a little down or like I'm stuck. They remind me to stay positive and keep believing in myself.

Catchphrases are little phrases that you can repeat. Think of superheroes. They have things that they say all the time, right? It's time for you to come up with your very own superhero catchphrase too. Here are some examples to get you started:

- I can do things even when they're hard!

- I always try my best and that's what matters!

- I can do it. I *will* do it.

- I believe in myself no matter what comes my way.

Say What You Think—Kindly

Another part of empowering yourself is knowing that you matter. What you think matters. When you think or feel something, it's good to talk about it. You should talk about it when someone or something bothers you. Oliver talked to his mom about how he felt and she helped him feel better.

One thing to remember is that when you share what you think, it's important to do it kindly.

You've probably heard of the Golden Rule: It's important to treat other people how you want to be treated.

If your brother or sister is annoying you, it's okay to tell them that they are. It's not okay to call them names. You can't say something like, "You're so annoying! I wish you were never born!" That's not nice. Talking like that isn't going to help solve your problem and is going to hurt the other person.

Instead, you should talk about how you feel without saying things that blame the other person. You could say, "When you poke me, it makes me feel really annoyed. Please give me my personal space." This way, you aren't being mean. You're saying how you feel.

Conclusion

Look at that, buddy!

You made it to the end! That deserves a pat on the back and a high five. You should be proud! You have learned about so many new things and gotten so many different ideas to help you grow.

Don't forget that every day is a chance to learn. It's a chance to practice those new skills so you can get better at them. When you're growing up, you're learning all about how to be a good adult. These skills will help you now and later.

You have a Champion Mindset in you. If it doesn't feel like it, you just need to remind yourself of it. Remember your catchphrases. Think about the things you do well and how hard you try. Be proud of yourself for learning and growing.

If you're ever stuck or you need help, your grown-ups are there to help you. They can walk you through the things that are hard. They can tell you stories about how they learned what you're trying to do. They can connect with you and help you learn how to fix your mistakes. Soon, those things that you made mistakes on today will be easier. Soon, you'll look back at the things that challenge you now and think, *Wow, that's so easy now!* That's when you'll know that you're growing.

Thanks for reading and I hope you had lots of fun along this journey.

See you in next year's edition of the Life Skills series!

Don't forget your free gifts!

(My way of saying thank you for your support)

Simply visit **haydenfoxmedia.com** to receive the following:

- 10 Powerful Dinner Conversations To Create Amazing Kids

- 10 Magical Affirmations To Help Kids Become Unstoppable in Life

(you can also scan this QR code)

More titles you're sure to love!

HAYDEN FOX

Made in the USA
Las Vegas, NV
15 December 2023

82910510R00059